W9-CCW-194

Together Again
Kinship of Word and Deed

Roger S. Greenway

MARC
800 West Chestnut Avenue, Monrovia, California 91016-3198

Together Again: Kinship of Word and Deed
Roger S. Greenway
ISBN 1-887983-08-02

Published by MARC, a division of World Vision International, 800 West Chestnut Avenue, Monrovia, California 91016-3198, U.S.A. in cooperation with the Evangelical Fellowship of Mission Agencies (EFMA), Atlanta, Georgia, and the Association of Evangelical Relief and Development Organizations (AERDO), Washington, D.C.

Part 1

The Foundation of Kinship: Theology of holism

Let me tell you an allegory about a man by the name of Christopher Prince. Prince founded a company called Prince Enterprise, which grew into a large, international business. Prince had two sons, whom he loved very much, and his intention was to see his sons working with him in Prince Enterprise.

All went well as the two boys grew up. They got along with each other and they shared the same vision of working with their father in managing and expanding Prince Enterprise. But it so happened that when the young men went off to college, and later to graduate school, they chose different institutions. The father hoped that the different orientations his sons received would enhance their participation in Prince Enterprise. But this did not prove to be the case.

As it turned out, Prince's sons learned two different approaches to doing business. They learned to set different goals. Their schools taught them different values. They both studied international business, but they learned different ways of organizing workers, predicting outcomes, reporting earnings and evaluating their work and accomplishments. Upon graduating from their respective schools, both sons wanted to go to work with their father in Prince Enterprise. But they found it difficult, in fact impossible, to work harmoniously with each other.

"Dad," they said, "we both want to work for you. We both want to be part of Prince Enterprise. Our loyalty to you and to the family is beyond question. But you will have to let us organize separate divisions of the company. We must each have our own particular assignments within the company. We will need separate offices. We have chosen different management structures, and each of

Roger S. Greenway is professor of world missiology at Calvin Theological Seminary, Grand Rapids, Michigan. A former missionary in Sri Lanka and Mexico, he was among the first to call the mission community to address the challenge of the world's great cities. He is a former director of the department of world ministries of the Christian Reformed Church. This publication is adapted from two presentations given at the joint executive forum of the Evangelical Fellowship of Mission Agencies (EFMA) and the Association of Evangelical Relief and Development Agencies (AERDO), at Glen Eyrie, Colorado Springs, Colorado, September 15-18, 1997.

us has to have authority to control our separate activities. Otherwise we will constantly be in each other's hair, and we know you don't want that. We will each report to you, but you will have to allow us to use different reporting systems. And of course, we'll keep separate financial accounts.

"You understand, Father," the sons said, "that we expect to produce different products, though hopefully they will be compatible. We love Prince Enterprise. We will always uphold the company name. But at the same time we need to be free to carry out our separate programs. Oh yes, we want to be free to enter into joint ventures with different overseas partners too."

The father knew that his sons loved Prince Enterprise, the company that he had sacrificed so much to establish. And they intended to be loyal to him and the family. But he also knew how independent and strong-minded his sons were, and how determined each of them was to prove his own importance. So the father let them have their way. Each son established a separate division of Prince Enterprise. The father hoped that eventually they would come together, do their planning together, coordinate their efforts, adopt the same goals and work with the same values. But he accepted the fact that for some time, Prince Enterprise would be a divided house.

Time passed. Both divisions of the company prospered. Each developed its own line of products, and each had its own investors and clients. Each developed its own corporate philosophy and management system. As could be expected, some tensions developed between the brothers and between their separate divisions of the company. They tried to keep the tensions hidden, because after all they were brothers and both were part of their father's company, Prince Enterprise. It wouldn't be good for business if clients heard about their disagreements.

The brothers were kept very busy in their separate offices, managing their separate affairs. They traveled overseas a great deal to visit subsidiaries in other countries and meet with their clients. Sometimes they'd run into each other at airports, but they never had time to talk seriously with each other, except at family get-togethers and occasionally at an executive-level conference. On company matters, each communicated directly with their father, but seldom with each other. And sometimes they could be heard talking against each other.

Years passed, and then one day the brothers met at a beautiful resort. "How are things going?" one asked the other. "Great," his brother responded with a smile. But after a pause he added, "Sometimes I think we're missing something. It's something Dad taught us when we were growing up but somehow we've forgotten.

"Years ago, before you and I split up, Dad had it all together. The company didn't have separate divisions, each going its own way. There wasn't any competition between one branch and the other. There was one main office, one plan, one set of company goals, and one accounting system. When anyone said 'Prince Enterprise,' they thought of one company. It sure made a lot of sense."

A long silence followed. It had taken years to bring the brothers to this moment. They were kin, with one father, working for the same company, but they hadn't acted like it. Oftentimes they hadn't felt like it either.

Moments passed that seemed like hours. Then the other brother nodded and said softly, "I've been thinking the same thing. Maybe it's time to put Prince Enterprise back together. Let's go talk to Dad." The brothers looked at each other, hardly believing what they had just said. Hardened attitudes of long standing had begun to change.

A short time later, when the father saw his two sons walking toward his office he noticed something different. Neither son was trying to get ahead of the other. Before a word was spoken, the father guessed what they had come for. His heart leaped for joy. Prince Enterprise was going to be together again.

A fundamental missiological question

The central truth of Christianity, to which all of us are committed, is that the God of the Bible, out of sheer love and grace has intervened in this fallen, fractured and suffering world, and through Jesus Christ his Son has redeemed lost sinners and reconciles them to himself through the gospel; and by his Spirit he is establishing a new order in this world. Jesus called the new order the "kingdom of God." In this kingdom, Jesus is the King and kingdom workers are his disciples. His disciples, those kingdom workers, are concerned about many things:

1) Proclamation of God's Word, calling people to repentance and faith,

2) Demonstration of love, compassion toward the poor, and righteousness in society,

3) Responsible exercise of stewardship toward creation and its precious God-given resources,

4) Spiritual warfare against Satan's dark kingdom, which has its tentacles everywhere—in individuals, communities and the power structures that control much of the world.

Speaking boldly and inclusively, kingdom ministries are services rendered in any or all these areas. Their ultimate goal is to glorify God and advance his kingdom by defending and practicing love, truth and righteousness in a sinful world. All these dimensions of kingdom ministry are closely intertwined. All will be needed until Christ returns and all things are made new (Rev. 21:1-4). [1]

I assume that among us this foundational position is not in question. What is in question is whether at this time we who are engaged in kingdom work can recover the unity we lost in the past fifty years, and can regain the wholeness and the efficacy of a common mission. To consider this question is the main purpose of our conference. The value of our discussions will be measured by what we do in the days to come.

Overview

Let me at this point give you a brief overview of what I was asked to do in these two presentations. Part I focuses on the biblical and the theological basis for "kinly" togetherness in holistic ministry. I will focus particularly on two areas: the relationship of evangelism and church development to relief and development. I can only touch lightly on the areas of stewardship of creation and spiritual warfare. Part 2 will address the demands, the obstacles and the hurdles we will have to overcome if we are to demonstrate that we are brothers and sisters with the same Father and serve his enterprise, the kingdom of God. We begin with a look at the Old Testament.

Together in the Old Testament

All dimensions of Israel's life and mission were clearly together in the Old Testament. Among all the nations and kingdoms of the ancient world, with their countless gods and pagan practices, Israel was a kingdom composed of people who were chosen by God to be witnesses to him. In the laws of Israel the nations could see how the one true God wanted to be worshiped, how a just society should be ordered, and how the resources of the earth should be managed for the common good.

From the writings of Moses to those of the psalmists, to the teachers of wisdom, to the early and later prophets, one thing was made clear: There was only one God. He alone was to be worshiped and he had carefully prescribed, in the laws of the covenant, the way in which he chose to be worshiped and served. The entire life of Israel as a theocratic kingdom was meant to be a covenant-keeping life. Every aspect of life was to be lived for God's glory, and all human relationships and activities were governed by God's law.

The laws of the covenant were regarded as holy laws. By keeping them the people would be holy and pleasing to God. God's laws set the standards of justice and righteousness in all human relationships, including the treatment of foreigners and sojourners. God's laws provided for the proper care of the soil, the rotation of crops, and rights of ownership. By means of his laws, God graciously gave Israel the knowledge, values and standards that they needed to worship him rightly and to live healthy, balanced lives that would honor God and benefit themselves and others. By keeping God's covenant Israel would fulfill its mission, which was to be a kingdom-on-display, a people set apart for others to look at and learn. Israel was to be a continual witness to all other kingdoms as to the nature of the one true God, Maker of heaven and earth, and his will for human conduct.[2]

The Old Testament makes it abundantly clear that care for the poor and the protection of the innocent against injustice were essential elements in the covenant life of the kingdom. The destitute and disabled, widows, orphans and sojourners were in fact singled out by Old Testament writers as worthy of and in need of special consideration by God's people. [3] In Exodus 21-33, which is often called the Book of the Covenant, we find the oldest prescriptions on covenantal responsibility. God said to his people:

- Do not mistreat an alien or oppress him, for you were aliens in Egypt (Ex. 22:31).

- Do not take advantage of a widow or orphan. If you do and they cry out to me, I will certainly hear their cry (Ex. 22:22-23).

- Do not deny justice to your poor people in their lawsuits (Ex. 23:6).

After Moses, the sermons and writings of the prophets sounded the same notes. The prophet Amos, for example, condemned the whole nation for its heartless treatment of the poor and the oppressed:

For three sins of Israel, even for four, I will not turn back (wrath). They sell... the needy for a pair of sandals. They trample on the heads of the poor... and deny justice to the oppressed (Amos 2:6-7).

Amos singled out the unrighteous judges (5:12), the profiteering businessmen (8:6) and the pleasure-seeking women of Samaria ("cows of Bashan," 4:1) as those that "trample the poor" (2:7; 5:11), "crush the needy" (4:1), and buy or sell the poor with silver or a pair of sandals (2:6; 8:6). [4]

The great prophet, Isaiah, from whom we learn so much about the forthcoming Messiah, spoke against Israel like a prosecuting attorney. Isaiah charged:
Your rulers are rebels, companions of thieves; they all love bribes and chase after gifts. They do not defend the cause of the fatherless; the widow's case does not come before them (1:23).

Isaiah challenged Israel's leaders to:

Stop doing wrong, learn to do right! Seek justice, encourage the oppressed. Defend the cause of the fatherless, plead the case of the widow (1:16-17).

The prophets were not inventing new moral codes. Rather, they were speaking as representatives of Israel's true King—the Lord God who stood for truth, compassion and righteousness. The prophets warned, exhorted and threatened judgment, because they knew that neglect of covenant obligations meant denying God and would result in divine punishment.

Many Old Testament passages can be cited, but one deserves special attention. In Jeremiah 21:11-23, the prophet contrasts King Jehoiakim's corrupt reign with that of his father, the good King Josiah. Here the prophet makes an important statement about what it means to know God. Addressing Jehoiakim, Jeremiah says:

Woe to him who builds his palace by unrighteousness, his upper rooms by injustice, making his countrymen work for nothing, not paying them for their labor... Does it make you (Jehoiakim) a king to have more and more cedar? Did not your father (Josiah) have food and drink? He did what was right and just, so all went well with him. He defended the cause of the poor and needy, and so all went well. Is that not what it means to know me? declares the Lord. (Jer. 22:13-16)

In these verses, King Jehoiakim was judged, Josiah was praised, and God's people instructed in what it meant to know the Lord. To "know the Lord" was to pursue justice for the poor.

Like other prophets, Jeremiah took the position that the absence of justice was a sure indication people lacked knowledge of the Lord. Israel's leaders, above all, were to be champions of the poor and the oppressed, and the people as a whole could be expected to follow their leaders' example. The virtue of concern for the poor was to characterize kings and citizens alike.[5]

I realize this Old Testament material is familiar to us. We have read it and heard it, many times before. Yet I feel that given the history of tensions and debates among us evangelicals, we need periodic reminders that holism is biblical. In fact, the Scriptures offer us no other option. From the beginning, the Bible has taught that covenant people, citizens of God's kingdom, are concerned about truth, love and righteousness, because God is concerned about them. We are kingdom people who know the Lord and show it in ways that the Bible clearly lays out.

The kind of dualism that separates the physical and the spiritual, word and deed, was not found in Old Testament theology. In the Old Testament, theology and ethics were bound together in the same law. Israelites could not with integrity announce the name of the Lord if they did not demonstrate in their lives mercy and justice as the Lord required.

This unity of theology and ethics was essential to Israel's mission to be a showcase kingdom among the nations. In the whole ancient world there was no other deity like the God of Israel, whose character was that of mercy, justice and redemption. In the pantheon of the gods there were vicious power struggles, petty quarrels, gross sexual behavior and countless other things that made the gods of the nations unfit models for human community. But Israel's God was different. He alone could say, "Be holy because I, the Lord your God, am holy" (Lev. 19:1).

The God to whom Israel bore witness was a God who was mighty to save from bondage, a God whose worship and service involved high ethical standards, and a God who cared about the poor and the oppressed. To those who knew him, his character was the highest motivation for holy living, and to anyone, anywhere, who truly sought righteousness the laws of his covenant were a shining light. Israel's high calling was to bear witness to such a God. Speaking for God, Isaiah wrote:

> I, even I, am the Lord, and apart from me there is no savior.
> I have revealed and saved and proclaimed—I, and not some
> foreign god among you. You are my witnesses, declares
> the Lord, that I am God. (Isa. 43:11-12)

Together in the New Testament

Israel failed the Lord in many ways. This grieved the prophets greatly. But still the prophet Jeremiah foresaw a day coming when God's covenant would be renewed and a people raised up whose minds would be quickened by the Spirit of God. They would return to the foundations of kingdom life and witness. Freed from sin's bondage through the atoning work of Messiah, they would apply themselves to their covenant obligations with joy and exuberance.

> "The time is coming, declares the Lord, when I will put
> mylaw in their minds and write them on their hearts.
> I will be their God, and they will be my people. No longer
> will a man teach his neighbor, or a man his brother, saying
> 'Know the Lord,' because they will all know me, from the
> least of them to the greatest." (Jer. 31:31ff)

Jeremiah expresses his point in a very forceful way here: What does it mean to know the Lord? It is to do what is just and right, and to defend the cause of the poor (Jer. 22:15-16). This, says the New Testament writer of Hebrews, is precisely what characterizes the "new covenant" community, the kingdom of our Lord and Savior Jesus Christ. This kingdom consists of men and women, boys and girls who know the Lord. They have seen his face in Jesus. They know him who is both Creator and Redeemer, the Holy One, the God who shows compassion on the needy and defends the oppressed. Knowing him, new covenant people become like him. Washed in Christ's blood they yield themselves to doing God's will (Heb. 10:15-18).

In Luke 4, we find the account of Jesus preaching in the synagogue at Nazareth. It was there that Jesus announced the commencement of the new era that began with him and his ministry. Jesus himself was the fulfillment of everything Israel was called to be and do. Subsequently, the mission of the church would flow from Christ's own messianic mission.

In the story as we find it in Luke 4, Jesus had just completed a tour of Galilee "in the power of the Spirit," says verse 14, and news about him had spread everywhere. As was his custom, when the Sabbath came, Jesus went into the synagogue. He stood up to read the scripture, and the scroll that was handed to him contained the writings of the prophet Isaiah, where it said:

> "The Spirit of the Lord is on me, because he has anointed me
> to preach good news to the poor. He has sent me to proclaim
> freedom for the prisoners and recovery of sight for the blind,
> to release the oppressed, to proclaim the year of the Lord's
> favor." (Isa. 61:1-2)

Having read this, Jesus rolled up the scroll, gave it back to the attendant. He began his sermon with the words: "Today this scripture is fulfilled in your hearing." This announcement by Jesus in Nazareth is one of the keys to our understanding of the essential unity of service and proclamation. Anointed by the Holy Spirit, Jesus spoke of a gospel that was at one and the same time good news spiritually, socially, emotionally and physically. It proclaimed good news to the poor, freedom for prisoners, and sight to the blind. When he called it the "year of the Lord's favor," he was saying that a new stage in the unfolding of the kingdom of God was at hand. In God's redemptive plan the floodgates of grace were now open to all nations, and henceforth people everywhere would be called to repent, believe and enjoy the blessings of God's kingdom and the challenges of its service.

Someone may ask, "Did the early believers understand what we today call 'holism'?" Did the apostles and the early church understand the linkage between the verbal and the visible proclamation of the kingdom? I believe they did. They may have lacked the vocabulary we use, but understood the message. Acquainted as they were with the first-hand accounts of Jesus' preaching and healing ministry, they could not possibly have separated word and deed. The stories about Jesus that we read in the four Gospels were stories told over and over in their preaching. The apostles knew the character of Jesus, his message, and the way he ministered. Wherever the gospel was heralded, people heard what Jesus had said about the fallen stranger on the wayside and the "neighbor" who saved his life. They heard about blind men crying out for mercy, and Jesus healing them. And they heard about lepers grasping for one last thread of hope, and Jesus making them whole.[6]

If we evangelicals are to have solid biblical and theological foundations for holistic missions, we need to keep in mind the broad sweep and kingdom teaching throughout the Bible. The background of Old Testament life and teaching, plus the teaching and example of Jesus during his earthly ministry, are for new covenant people the source of instruction and continual inspiration. And as Jesus predicted, we are empowered to move beyond Old Testament Israel, because the Spirit of the Lord has written his laws upon our hearts and minds.

The personal changes that occur in people who have experienced regeneration and the indwelling of the Holy Spirit bear this out. Unless the impulses born of the Holy Spirit are suppressed by some evil influence, or are left to wither, unnourished by true and consistent instruction from the Word, regenerate people almost immediately start to look toward a lost and suffering world and begin to minister in Christ-like ways. They seek to lead old friends and relatives to Christ. They show concern for the poor and suffering. Evils that before their conversion they hardly even noticed now disturb them, and they try to correct them. In one area of life after another they seek to change what was bad into something good. What I am claiming here is not mere theory; it is historical fact, attested to repeatedly in the history of Christianity.

Let's examine the record: Over nineteen centuries, the church had it together. From the beginning of the New Testament church and its outreach to the world, the proclamation of the gospel and what today we call "community development" have gone hand in hand.[7] Acts 6 tells us that when widows from the Greek-speaking segment of the church at Jerusalem felt neglected in the daily distribution of food, seven men with Greek names were appointed to take care of them (Acts 6:1-6).

The apostle Paul, whose primary gifts and calling lay in evangelism and church planting, was involved in collecting funds for the poor and transporting relief money to believers who were in need (Rom. 15:25-28; 1 Cor. 8:19-20). During his ministry at Ephesus, Paul worked with his hands in order to supply his own needs and the needs of his fellow workers, and to help the poor (Acts 20:34-45).

The world in which the early church grew and thrived was struck with awe at the love and sacrifice shown by Christians. Christians not only preached the gospel, at personal expense and often at risk of their lives, they cared for orphans and abandoned children, they brought food to prisoners, nursed the sick and in times of plague, buried the dead, including strangers. One of the key reasons why the gospel made such an appeal in the first three centuries lay in the fact that Christians addressed the urgent needs and problems of the day in practical ways. They thereby demonstrated that citizens of Christ's kingdom had a new life within them, a life that showed itself by making positive contributions to the welfare of society.

This same pattern has been repeated throughout history. From the fourth to the eighteenth century, nearly all missionaries were monks. While the original purpose of monasticism was not missionary, but grew out of the desire for the spiritual renewal of the church, most monastic movements became missionary in the course of time. Some were ardently missionary, like the Nestorians who spread east into Arabia, India and across central Asia into China; and the Celts, who arose in Ireland and moved into Scotland and England and across central Europe; followed later by the Franciscans, Dominicans and Jesuits.

These communities of monks functioned as both missionaries of the gospel, and promoters and preservers of civilization in places where warfare and chaos had reigned for years. Monks promoted education, especially literacy, and a better way of life based on agriculture, more advanced technology, discipline, hard work and Christian faith and morality. Almost everywhere, monasteries became centers of religion, education and civilization.[8] As best they could with the resources of their times, the monks held it all together, word and deed, down to the beginning of the modern period.

Four Movements - All four of the early Protestant renewal movements were what we today would call "holistic" in their approach. All four made an impact on Protestant missions later on.

1. Puritanism

The puritans aimed at "purifying" the Church of England along more Calvinistic lines. It was among these Puritans that Protestant missionary theology first developed in the English-speaking world.[9] The two greatest Puritan advocates of missions were Richard Baxter, a pastor in England and John Eliot, who became a missionary among American Indians.

The life of Eliot and other missionaries like him has been described in the following way. He (Eliot) traveled on foot and horseback, taxing his strength to the utmost, sometimes drenched for days at a time, all to bring the gospel to the natives. He brought cases to court to prevent defrauding of Indian land, pleaded clemency for convicted Indian prisoners, fought the selling of Indians into slavery, sought to secure lands and streams for Indian use, established schools for Indian children and adults, translated books, and attempted to show a deep humanitarianism that accompanied their concern for salvation.[10] That certainly sounds holistic.

2. Pietism

In Germany, the church was dominated by the state and spirituality was at a low ebb. Philip Jacob Spener, influenced by Puritan writers, published in 1675 a book in which he presented suggestions for the renewal of the church. These suggestions included:

(1) more use of the Word of God,

(2) a more diligent exercise of spiritual priesthood by all believers, and

(3) the obligation of all believers not only to confess true religion with their mouths, but to practice it by acts of love and compassion, following the example of the Good Samaritan in the parable of Jesus.

All the great Pietist leaders—August H. Francke, George Mueller and Bartholomew Ziegenbalg—maintained Spener's well-rounded emphases, including his insistence on a comprehensive approach to ministry and missions. Besides preaching the gospel and building churches, Pietists built schools so that children and adults might learn to read. They healed the sick as best they could with the medical knowledge of their day, and they built and maintained orphanages, they opposed cruelty and injustice, they sought to bring peace between warring groups, and they promoted legislation to end social evils. No one could ever charge the Pietists with not having word and deed together.[11]

3. Moravianism

The Moravians sprang from German Pietism and had roots that went back even before the Reformation. Moravians were one of the most remarkable missionary movements in history. They were intensely devoted to prayer, evangelism, and sending missionaries to distant lands, and especially to American Indians. Their missionary approach was holistic. Wherever they became established the Moravians taught local people improved agricultural techniques, horticulture, animal husbandry and ways to engage in trade.[12] Within the limitations of their times, the Moravians kept word and deed together.

4. The Wesleyans

The fourth movement that flowed into the modern Protestant missionary movement was the Wesleyan revival that came out of Anglicanism in England. The Wesleyan revival was closely associated with the great awakenings in North America that were themselves outgrowths of Puritanism.[13]

Both streams were concerned about evangelism and the needs of the poor and destitute. Unquestionably, John Wesley focused on preaching. He preached some 45,000 sermons and published more than 200 books and pamphlets. He organized cell groups for prayer and Christian nurture. However, he also started the first free dispensary in England for medical assistance to the poor. Wesley organized the Friends Society to give emergency aid to strangers. He supported efforts to provide elementary education to children of the poor. He vigorously opposed the slave trade and promoted prison reform. All this from a man who was first of all a preacher.

Likewise, the great preacher and evangelist, George Whitefield, spoke out against the cruel and inhumane treatment of slaves. Whitefield raised money for orphanages and insisted that Christians work for the betterment of human society at all levels.

As a result of these movements and the influence of great evangelical leaders, eventually there came many organized efforts such as Sunday schools, orphanages, homes for "fallen girls" as they were called, and rescue missions. In every case, the goals were to minister to the lost and needy by means of evangelism and social action together.

The Modern Missionary Movement

William Carey is generally referred to as the "father of the Protestant missionary movement." Many Protestant missionaries preceded him, of course. But without question, Carey lighted a fire that spread to every corner of the Protestant world and set in motion the modern missionary movement. And who was more holistic in his missionary approach than William Carey?

Carey addressed the challenges of presenting Christ to the Hindu world from every possible angle. He learned several Indian languages, and preached in them. He supervised the translation of the Scriptures, established schools, introduced advanced methods of agriculture and horticulture, attacked the inhuman treatment of lepers who were often burned to death or buried alive. Carey campaigned against infanticide and the burning of widows, until both evils were officially prohibited by the colonial government.

Carey's pattern was followed by most Protestant missions throughout the nineteenth century and the early twentieth centuries. Beside setting up and staffing schools, hospitals and clinics, missionaries introduced improved methods of agriculture. They were involved in countless things that today we would call "community development." Some missionaries exposed themselves to slander and violence by fighting the slave trade, traffic in opium, the exploitation of children in mines and other industries, and prostitution.

Besides all these things, no force was more influential in raising the status of women than the missionary movement. In places where women had no rights, were never allowed to go to school or learn to read and write, missionaries came in and evangelized women. They helped women learn to read, and taught them to see themselves as children of God.[14] This dynamic influence continues today in places where the gospel is just now entering.

The Great Reversal

Now we have to ask: With such a holistic heritage behind us, what happened in the twentieth century to drive a wedge between evangelism and social concern? One writer, Linda Smith, calls it the "great reversal." She says:

> The early 1900s brought great upheaval among Christians in America. Kantian philosophy, Darwinism, the rise of sociology and psychology, new understandings of science, and new ways of examining the Bible based on analyses of historical and literary contexts were perceived as threatening basic beliefs about the nature of reality, human nature, God's role in creation, the nature of the Bible and historicity of Jesus and his miracles.[15]

As a backlash against liberalism, the inheritors of the evangelical tradition went into a period of retreat and separatism which had a profound impact on their social concern. All progressive social concern was nearly eliminated among evangelicals by the end of the 1900-1930 period.

George Marsden, one of the foremost historians of evangelicalism, attributes the decline of private social concern to the increasing stigma caused by the Social Gospel, which was in its zenith during the first three decades of the 20th century and was strongly identified with theological liberalism. The Social Gospel emphasized Christian obligation to respond to physical need and oppression, the priority of social action and the task of establishing the kingdom of God on earth now through human efforts. Fundamentalists rejected these and emphasized spiritual need, evangelism and the future heavenly aspects of the kingdom of God. Theological conservatives began to rigidly dichotomize evangelism and social concern, word and deed.

Following Marsden's lead, Smith goes on to say that while historically word and deed had been held tightly together in evangelical missions, now the strong negative reaction against liberal theology, and especially against the Social Gospel, had a depressing effect on the fundamentalists' attitude toward social ministries of any kind other than "emergency" relief. In an effort to avoid the dangerous mistakes of liberalism, American fundamentalists, and many of their evangelical offspring, abandoned a vital part of their own beliefs and historic tradition.[16]

The effects of the Great Reversal spilled over into mission structures and organizations. Divisions occurred within the evangelical family which led in the second half of the twentieth century to the creation of many new and separate agencies. Some emphasized evangelism and others focused on social needs. Separate missiologies developed, with books and articles promoting each of them. Overlapping overseas programs appeared with their own administrations, goals and methods. Consequently, competition for funds developed, as each program and agency developed its own supporting constituency. Overseas, each agency developed its own set of partners. The result was that a confusing image of the whole missions enterprise emerged.

Worst of all, there occurred a tearing asunder of something the kingdom of God intended to be united visibly and actually. The holism of the kingdom vision became garbled. Kingdom ministries that were supposed to be integrated so as to address spiritual and social needs in a unified way were turned into a circus of competing priorities and organizations.

Some of us feel that much of the malaise that missions is currently experiencing in some places, and some of our financial problems as well, are prices we pay for the mistakes of the past. Yet we cling to old ideas and dichotomized structures, though the warning signals multiply around us.

I believe it is time for us to awaken to the fact that many younger people in our churches are catching a holistic vision for the kingdom. They are looking for new paradigms that demonstrate an integrated approach to kingdom ministry.

With that in mind I will address in Part 2 what I consider to be the burning question we must answer if this meeting is to amount do something more than shop talk. The question is: What must we "kin" folk do to go get together? Are we willing to pay the price of collaboration, maybe of merger, so as to advance

God's kingdom in a more biblical and holistic way in a world where resources are limited, time is short and the poor and the lost are so many? Are we willing to do what it takes to overcome the differences that keep us apart?

Part 2

The Cost of Kinship

Recently my wife and I visited our daughter, Kathy, and her husband, Jeff, and their four boys in the Dominican Republic. While we were there they celebrated the fourteenth anniversary of their arrival in that country and the beginning of their evangelistic and educational ministry among the country's poorest children, the children of the Haitian cane cutters who live in scattered villages called "bateys." From the outset, their goal was to establish a school along with every church so that the children might receive a Christ-centered education and someday escape the grinding poverty and inhumane treatment of the cane cutter's life.

The Lord has wonderfully blessed their efforts. Since 1983 the program has grown from one school with 30 pupils to 35 schools with nearly 4,000 pupils. All the teachers are local men and women, most of them trained by the mission's own teacher development program.

As to the impact of the Christian schools on the growth of the churches, just ask the pastors. Pastors clamor for more schools because they see what the schools do for their members. For more than a decade, not one of the young people that went through the Christian schools has had to take up cane cutting to earn a living. To the people in the bateys, a school and church together offer Christ-centered hope that former generations never knew.

About three years ago, one of the Christian school teachers, Julio, became seriously ill. Earlier he had hepatitis and had received several blood transfusions, and he soon died of AIDS. Julio's death was mourned by the village church, by the Christian school where he had been a teacher, and by his widow, Mariluz and their two sons. A year later the younger of the sons died, also of AIDS. This left Mariluz with one boy, six-year-old Benjamin.

It was a year ago last May that Mariluz, thin and wasted by the disease that now ravished her body, appeared without notice at the door of our daughter, Kathy, in Santo Domingo. Next to Mariluz stood her one remaining child, six-year-old Benjamin.

"I'm dying," she said to Kathy, "and I'm asking you to take Benjamin. I'm all he's got. Nobody in the family will take him. They are all afraid because they think he has AIDS. Will you take him... and make him your son?"

During the next few days Kathy and Jeff did some fervent praying. What did God want them to do? They already had three sons, the youngest about Benjamin's age. Benjamin might very well be HIV-positive. His father had died of AIDS two years earlier; his little brother shortly after that, and now his mother was dying of the disease.

Should they first have Benjamin tested for HIV, and then make a decision as to whether to take him? Or should the risk of AIDS not even be a factor in their decision?

A few days later, after much emotional and spiritual wrestling, they came to a decision. They would take Benjamin whether he was HIV-positive or not. When Benjamin's mother heard their decision, she immediately turned the boy over to them. She gave Kathy and Jeff a legal document, already notarized, stating that she wanted Benjamin adopted by them. A week later, Mariluz died.

All that is now history. Benjamin has been tested three times for HIV, and thankfully the test results are negative. Like all adoptive parents, Kathy and Jeff now face the challenge of meeting Benjamin's special needs. He has some deep wounds which only time, love and divine grace will heal. The family's goal is to help Benjamin develop in every way into the kind of person God wants him to be.

Their plans for the boy are shaped by the goals and values of the kingdom of God. The spirit of that kingdom is love. When you love a child biblically, you see that child as a precious image-bearer of God. This immediately makes you concerned about all dimensions of the child's well-being—physical, emotional, educational and religious.[17] That is holistic love. Anything less than that is sub-Christian and a deception.

What kind of parents would they be if they decided to reduce their stress by drawing certain lines and staying within them. For instance, what if they would provide Benjamin with food, clothing and a bed to sleep in, but would not send him to school and would keep religion out of the picture? What if they left it up to Benjamin whether he chose to inquire about God or go to church? Or what if in certain areas they set high goals for Benjamin and monitored his development carefully, but treated him more as a project than a person, and withheld the love and security of intimate personal relationships?

What if they told Benjamin: "We intend to help you until you are eighteen, but after that you are on your own. Don't come back to us if you run into trouble. Find someone else to help you."

We all know the answers to these questions. By taking Benjamin, Kathy and Jeff made a commitment that is comprehensive and long-term. It cannot be reduced to quick-fix solutions designed to get the boy off their hands as quickly as possible.

They have taken as their goal the development of a human being into a useful citizen of God's kingdom. For that goal to be achieved, the love and nurture they give must be multi-dimensional and of one piece. Christ must be at its center. It must embrace Benjamin's spiritual needs and also his physical, mental and emotional needs. Neither in the home, nor in the church or the community can love and nurture be carved into pieces and compartmentalized without losing their power and integrity.

Of course we realize that there are differences between parenting a child and evangelizing, making disciples, planting churches and developing communities. But there are also parallels, and reductionism is always a serious temptation. Making disciples and developing communities must both be undertaken holistically, because they are motivated by the same comprehensive love and are manifestations of the one kingdom of Jesus Christ who came to save people, people made in God's image, people with bodies, minds, emotions and eternal souls.

The driving force in all our ministries is love, and love is holistic or it isn't love at all. Genuine love cannot be reduced to one facet of human well-being while others are ignored. Love does not permit its diverse and multiple applications to be segregated or compartmentalized. On the contrary, love wraps them together in one dynamic whole with Christ at the center. And of such is the kingdom of God.

The Big Questions

Having said this, we turn to the questions that I posed at the close of yesterday's presentation: What must we "kin" folk do to advance God's kingdom in a holistic manner, and are we willing to pay the price of changing our reductionistic ways and removing barriers that have kept us and our ministries apart?

The price, I believe, is as high and perhaps for many of us as painful as repentance itself. "Repentance" is not a popular idea for any of us. But I believe that nothing short of humble repentance is what is needed if we are going to remove the difficulties. I mean by "repentance" a profound change of attitude based on a new vision of kingdom servanthood. I invite you to consider with me the particular form of repentance required in four areas.

1.   We need to repent of our dichotomizing between "word" and "deed" in evangelical missiology and return to the holism of the kingdom that is plainly biblical.

Dr. Craig Ellison, who teaches Missiology at Nyack Seminary in Nyack, New York, points out that "most of us in Western society have Greek minds." [18] He means to say that our way of thinking focuses on analysis. Science and technology depend on this kind of thinking. We are trained to divide the whole into parts and treat the parts as though they existed independently from each other and from their context. This is the Greek way of thinking about reality. "Because of our Greek-mindedness," says Ellison, "we talk about spirit, mind, emotions and body as though these intricately interrelated dimensions of the person can be separated and adequately addressed in isolation." [19]

This segmented view of human beings affects our practice of Christian missions. Those of us that are preachers and evangelists direct all or most of our energies toward the spiritual side of people. We leave the other dimensions, the physical and psychological, to other "specialists," who often are secularists. Ellison points out that this segmented way of thinking about people is not the biblical way, as we were reminded yesterday in our review of the Old Testament writings.

Says Ellison:

> "Greek mindedness is dramatically different from the Hebraic or Old Testament orientation, which sees people as a whole. Hebraic thinking focuses on fusion rather than fission, synthesis rather than analysis, intuition rather than empiricism, system rather than segment. It resists the kind of reductionism that makes people into less than what God created them to be, whether it is the reductionism of secularism or the reductionism of fundamentalism.[20]

> If we are to make any significant progress in bringing back together word and deed ministries, we will have to address the missiological issues arising from our reductionistic and segmented way of thinking about people and their needs. We must learn to see people as complex, whole beings, because that is the way God created us and that is how he is redeeming us. Even our frail bodies, Ellison points out, will be eternally redeemed in incorruptible form (1 Cor. 15:42).[21] God obviously regards these bodies as precious."

This leads me to believe that we do not need a separate missiology of development, as distinct from a missiology of evangelism and church growth. There is just one *missio dei*. It is the mission of the kingdom. While kingdom mission embraces various dimensions of service and a variety of functions and applications, these are all intimately related to one another. They are intended to work together synergistically, and when we dichotomize them conceptually we set the stage for functional divisions that confuse our witness and weaken the Christian mission as a whole.

Such compartmentalization, in my opinion, has been a major weakness of evangelical missiology in the past fifty years. To say this, I realize, is tantamount in some circles to waving a red flag before a belligerent bull. Yet I sense that younger missiologists, particularly those from non-Western countries, are eager to see changes. Are we who have been so long identified with certain patterns of thought and ministry willing to admit that we may need to be corrected? Are we willing to pay the price of reconceptualizing evangelical missiology in terms of a more biblical holism?

2.   We must repent of the truncated vision and the narrow goal-setting which many of our organizations have invested in during the past forty years, and come to agreement on what the Lord has called us to do together.

I propose to both sides of the missionary family—relief and development workers, church planters and evangelists—that we agree on the following statement of a unified kingdom-focused missiology:

It is our understanding that the fulfillment of the Great Commission requires that we proclaim the gospel of Jesus Christ, plant and nurture churches, apply the principles of Christ's kingdom in all areas of community life (compassion, justice, stewardship), and seek to reclaim the whole cosmos (soil, water, air, minerals) from the control of Satan and his kingdom.

To that end we will proclaim the gospel of Christ's kingdom in words and deeds, accept suffering and if needs be persecution, in order that Christ's name be known, his Lordship over all of life acknowledged, and the love, truth, and righteousness of his kingdom spread everywhere.

In all that we do we will seek to gather a saved people, the church, and motivate and equip its members to be agents of transformation in terms of truth, love and justice in tangible ways in their communities and nations.

We affirm in our hearts and commit to showing in our lives that we are Christ's "kin-folk" and with Christ our goal is that God's glory will be revealed throughout the earth and his kingdom extended everywhere.

Can all of us sign off on that statement? If we can, then I see no reason why we cannot begin to take new steps of visible, operational togetherness. Collaboration based on a united commitment to kingdom values and perspective has great potential for the future. It will require, however, that with a repentant spirit we openly affirm ministries that in the past we played down. It means that henceforth we will embrace as vital and important colleagues in kingdom missions those that in the past we regarded as working for "the other side."

Are we willing to pay that price?

3.   We all need to take a closer look at ourselves and admit to the middle-class "captivity" of evangelical thinking about ministry among the poor, and repent.

It is uncommon, not to say uncomfortable, for leaders of evangelical agencies to admit that for the most part we are profoundly middle-class in our thinking. We have been educated in middle-class schools, we live in middle-class homes, and we attend middle-class churches where we listen to sermons delivered in middle-class language within the conceptual framework of middle-class people. And, admit it or not, when we engage in Christian ministry we approach the work with middle-class attitudes toward the poor, the needs of the poor, the message the poor need to hear, and the best strategies to help them. Worse yet, we are too ignorant to admit our own captivity to middle-class values, biases and methodologies.

A North American missiologist whom I admire for his insights on many issues is Bryant Myers. Myers works with World Vision and writes regularly in the "MARC Newsletter." In a recent article entitled "What Is Poverty Anyway?" Bryant tries to help middle-class evangelicals like us see the poor as they really are. He describes how broken relationships, oppressive political and economic systems, and cruel cultural patterns lie behind so much of poverty. If we sincerely want to operate holistically and help the poor by undoing the wrongs that keep them in misery, we will have to pay a high price.

Let's take a close look at the price tag.

Myers warns that if we challenge comfortable middle-class thinking and ways in regard to the poor, some people will get angry, including some who support our agencies. For, says Myers,

> The world cannot, and doesn't even want to transform political, economic, and social power into something that is pro-life, pro-poor and pro-kingdom. Sustainable change will not come through community organizing, political processes, or more education.

Challenging the poverty-creating nature of power will demand the transformational power of the gospel. It will be about personal sin and social sin. Only the Good News—all of it—contains the hope that the poor will someday be able to build homes and live in them. [22]

I hear in Myers' words a cry for integrated ministry, for an end to reductionism on the left and on the right, for the word of the gospel joined to honest efforts on behalf of the poor, and a willingness to sacrifice for the sake of both. I sense also an appeal for a repentant spirit, a humble admission that many of our efforts have not in the long run accomplished very much, and a confession that even we who say we serve the poor love power, whatever we have of it, when it works to our advantage.

Since I teach in a seminary, I cannot help but think of these academic citadels of middle-class values and theology where we train church leaders and a good number of missionaries. Bewailing the lack of understanding of the poor that he sees among church leaders and those who teach them, Harv Oostdyk points out that while exhaustive scholarship has been applied to uncover the precise etymology of the words of Scripture, and hundreds of books are written and published every year covering almost every area of theology, not much energy is extended to help church leaders understand the poor and how Scripture applies to them.[23]

Oostdyk observes that very few pastors and seminary professors have even rudimentary experience among the poor. They are "experientially deprived," he says, because they have spent most of their years in middle-class churches and seminary classrooms, but hardly ever in a ghetto. [24] "If every biblical scholar, student and preacher," says Oostdyk, "spent one month living among the poor, no church in America would ever be the same. Neither would any poor neighborhood." [25]

Are we willing to pay the price of relating personally to poor people? Dare we walk the streets they walk and sleep where they sleep? And can we expect other evangelical leaders to pay the price of becoming genuinely and consistently pro-poor with us?

The places in the world where the gospel is spreading fastest and church growth is by conversion, are the places where this "middle-class captivity" does not exist. In these "grass-roots" churches, members and leaders know from experience the nature of poverty. They do not need that anyone explain to them the importance of biblical holism. Nor do their pastors and leaders need conferences that argue for what the Bible so plainly teaches.

Some of the most effective holistic ministries I know are those that originate in the "grass-roots" churches of the Southern world. They operate without fanfare and in ways so down-to-earth that Western evangelicals would probably never think of them. But one thing characterizes all of them: word and deed are woven together. What God joined together in ancient times these "grass-roots" churches have not put asunder.

Can we humble ourselves to learn from them?

The fourth "repentance" addresses a number of attitudinal evils that have driven a wedge between kingdom workers and between their ministries for several decades. The only cure for these evils begins with repentance, and a profound change of attitude.

4. We must repent from:
   - The evil of our "priestly" tradition, which is the tradition of a clergy class controlling the church and its ministries;
   - The evil of "elitism" among missionaries that places one class of kingdom workers on a pedestal above others;
   - The evil of avoiding or muting the verbal presentation of the gospel and sometimes even arguing that "deed" ministries are enough by themselves;
   - The evil of avoiding the organized church overseas, or merely using the church when it serves our purpose, but not really taking the church seriously or seeking its best interests.
   - The evil of private "empire building," which has been a driving force behind many of the separate agencies begun in the past four decades.

Whenever a Christian relief and development worker serving overseas out of love for Christ and people is made to feel second-class among missionaries it is sin. Those who thrust such feeling on their colleagues need to repent, for their attitude is a hindrance and embarrassment to the kingdom of God.

Whenever relief and development workers conduct their activities without pointing people to Jesus and verbalizing the gospel in some way, they deny the Lord and his cross, and they should repent.

Whenever mission workers of any kind bypass the church they not only deprive their efforts of the best chance for long-term sustainability, they show an ungodly attitude toward the community for which Christ died. They need to repent.

Whenever we see in ourselves and in our organizations indications that crave for power and control, rivalry and competition, and the impulse to grow our own "empire" play a role in our agencies and in our planning for the future, we need to get down on our knees. Such things are not of God, but of the flesh and the devil.

5. We need to repent from practices and procedures that treat people as "clients" and which replace honest and durable relationships with a string of numerical goals, glowing reports and short-term solutions.

No one can do effective evangelism or establish durable churches, or carry on development work that has long-term sustainability, who operates out of a mindset that does not build, and continually maintain solid relationships, and networks of relationships, grounded on trust, shared values and common long-term commitments.

Over the past several decades I have seen many flash-in-the-pan operations among both community development workers and church planters. They followed a quick-fix approach that ignored on the one hand the complexity of human needs and on the other hand the central issue of salvation through Christ alone. This approach usually is the product of two evils: the first, of not taking Christ and the gospel seriously, and the second, of not taking people seriously, but instead treating people as "clients," or "projects" to be worked on until they reach a level that satisfies us, at which point we drop them.

Douglas and Judy Hall are two people I admire very much. For nearly four decades they have managed the Emmanuel Gospel Center (EGC) in inner-city Boston. Their ministry has always been kingdom-focused, blending emergency relief, social action, evangelism and church planting. EGC has helped to start and develop literally scores of multi-ethnic churches in the Boston area. At the same time, the mission has addressed almost every conceivable social need in the inner city.

The key to their ministry, says Douglas Hall, has been to focus on people and the long-term process of developing people and their communities rather than becoming overly product- or goal-oriented. Too often, says Hall, we who work for Christian organizations fall into a pattern of manipulating people in order to meet our own objectives. In our typical Western preoccupation with meeting our "goals," we forget the importance of human relationships without which neither strong churches nor long-term development is likely to be achieved. Unfortunately, says Hall, we are driven by a system that requires us to report that "last year we fed so many, or during the summer campaign we saw so many saved." [26]

When we become obsessively goal-oriented in our ministry, and when our goals are reductionistic rather than holistic, we easily fall into the trap of fragmenting people. We divide them into manageable and measurable pieces, and we assign each piece to this or that person or agency to offer the appropriate service. When we do that, people become our "clients." Personal respect and dignity, and relationship-building are lost, while we hasten to produce another glowing report of the numerical goals we achieved.

That is not the way Jesus worked. Nor has it ever led to long-term transformation of human beings and communities. It is not my intention to berate goal setting or belittle the insights of modern management. But many of us have become so obsessed with "results," "numbers," "progress reports" that we have disregarded certain fundamental truths that the Bible teaches and history repeatedly illustrates.

The kingdom of our Lord consists of people who know, love and serve the King, who is none other than Jesus the Savior revealed in Scripture and proclaimed by the word of the gospel. The citizens of his kingdom have a common spiritual center, namely Christ, and they share the values he teaches—unselfishness, accountability, compassion, justice and truth.

The first responsibility of kingdom workers is to represent their Lord honestly, accurately, and as completely as possible, not in some fragmented form, but as he is, the one Lord who offers to sinning, suffering human beings not only mercy to "die with dignity," (to use Mother Teresa's well-known phrase) but grace to live with dignity as sons and daughters of the one true God, and in the end to die at peace with him, and spend eternity with him because of Christ.

It is not the highest good we desire for ourselves, and should we seek anything less for others? Nothing short of that goal is worthy of the kingdom of God.

A Growing Convergence

My friends, to the extent to which we have lost that overarching kingdom vision, we need to repent and seek to regain the holism we somehow lost. We need to focus again on people, and on the transformational process that Jesus vividly described in his parables of the kingdom. Both the church world and the development world are riddled with sad examples of our mistakes. Of all people, we evangelicals should feel ashamed, because had we listened to the Scriptures and observed our Lord more attentively, we might have avoided many errors.

Today, however, I am optimistic. Because I see a growing concern that we regain lost ground and come together in new and more biblical ways. I see a growing awareness, evidenced by the agenda of this conference, that "kinship" must mean more than "spiritual" kinship. We must start to plan together, strategize holistically, and evaluate outcomes in terms of kingdom goals and values.

One of the encouraging signs of a growing convergence of visions and goals is the appearance of training programs, like that of Ted Yamamori, president of Food for the Hungry International and that of Bob Moffitt, president of Harvest. These programs train pastors and local congregations in methods of local ministry that are holistic, biblically balanced and whole-person focused.[27]

Further, I no longer sense opposition to two propositions that I formulated years ago and which in the beginning encountered resistance. The statements are these:

> If we wipe out poverty but neglect to tell the poor the Good News about Jesus Christ, we will have failed in our mission. And if we preach the gospel but ignore the plight of the poor, we are false prophets. Scripture supports both statements, and together they commit us to a unified ministry of word and deed in Christ's name. If ever they are separated, the overall witness of the gospel suffers.

Brothers and sisters, we are "kith and kin," and we need each other. We share the kingdom mission of showing and telling the world about God's love and grace. Let me illustrate from my own quite ridiculous experience what happens when the "show-ers" and the "tell-ers" aren't together.

I am basically a "preacher" type. Over the years I have been pulled into a variety of mission-related ministries, but I remain basically an evangelist and a church developer. I know little about agriculture and even less about things mechanical. Back in the 1950s at the old Kennedy School of Missions, I got some training in first aid tropical medicine and what to do when there was no doctor around. But other than that, I can't offer much.

However, wherever I planted churches, I tried to help people in tangible ways. Because I did not have a relief-and-development type co-worker, I made a lot of mistakes and really didn't help people very much.

During the decade of the 1960s, I helped plant a number of village churches among the Mazahua Indians in the mountains of the State of Michoacan, in southern Mexico. I worked closely with a Wycliffe Bible translator, Donald Stuart. Don was translating the New Testament into Mazahua, and we would go from village to village together. Don would read the Scriptures in Mazahua from his big blue notebook, and I would preach in Spanish. The Lord blessed and a string of new churches were organized.

The Mazahua villagers were terribly poor. Mothers and children were malnourished and as a result infant mortality was high. Vaccinations were unknown, and epidemics could wipe out a dozen children in a single night. None of the villages had electricity. They had no sewer system of any kind and securing safe drinking water was a major problem.

Despite my lack of technical know-how, I attempted various remedies. In one village I dug a well and brought in a pump. But it didn't work for very long. In another village I set up a gas-powered corn mill to make it easier and faster for the women to grind corn. But the men fought over the mill. Finally someone threw nails into the hopper and that ended its life.

My greatest success, if you could call it that, occurred when I launched a campaign against rats in the village of Rancho Viejo. Rats were everywhere, and they ate a large share of the villagers' corn crop.

One night in mid-September, when the corn had just been harvested, I made the mistake of placing my sleeping bag on the church floor near the corn offerings that the members had presented during the worship service the evening before. All night long I was kept awake by the sound of rats chomping away at the corn. Worst of all, some of the pesky fellows kept running back and forth over my sleeping bag. It was during that long, sleepless night that I declared war on the rat population.

But how to go about depleting the rat supply was a tough problem. I did not dare introduce rat poison, because children might eat it and become sick. Even a hundred traps would not do the trick. Then I notice that there was not a single cat in the village. Cats and dogs, of course, represented food and unless the villagers valued the animals for some service they might perform, they would soon end up on the dinner table. But, I reasoned, maybe the villagers would spare cats if they saw that cats ate rats, and without rats everyone would be better off.

It so happened that I knew a Christian couple that worked for a rich and eccentric old lady on the outskirts of Mexico City. This lady maintained an enormous kennel for stray cats and dogs. She had hundreds of the animals, all housed in neat, clean cages, and the animals ate better than did thousands of Mexican children. My friends, the caretakers of these privileged animals, agreed to supply me with 13 cats—12 pregnant females, and one healthy tom cat. One weekend I delivered the cats to the village. With prayers and solemn ceremony in which I explained the cats' mission, I turned over one cat each to 13 different families. Each family promised not to eat the cat, but to let the cat take care of the rats.

Well, it worked for a while. The next time I came to the village the cats had delivered their kittens. Young cats could be seen everywhere and the rat population seemed to be down. But about a year later, food supplies ran low and most of the cats disappeared. Nobody ever told me what happened, but I suspect the cats were eaten.

That is the kind of foolishness you get when a person like me tries to do relief and development without a skilled co-worker. Don Stewart was a linguist and a Bible translator; I was an evangelist and church planter. What we lacked was a team member who could have helped villagers like those in Rancho Viejo. Had we had such a person working alongside us, the villagers' grinding poverty might have been relieved, children's lives saved, churches strengthened and praises to God shouted by a thousand lips. Indeed, the kingdom of Jesus Christ did come to Rancho Viejo, and to other villages like it. But it might have come more holistically, with greater transforming power, and with more evidences of God's love, had a third person, a development worker, been part of our team. Synergism = "joint action for maximum effect." Interacting of elements that when combined produce a total effect than the sum of the individual contribution.

Symbiosis (or symbiotic) = "materialism." The living together of two dissimilar organisms interdependently, for mutual benefit.

My hope and prayer is that this conference will be the occasion when sons of the same Father will determine to take steps to bring together their mission efforts. If we work together "synergetically," as well as "symbiotically," we will mightily enhance each other's ministry. Together we will achieve far more than we could ever accomplish apart. [28]

Let's close the book on mistakes and divisions of the past 50 years, and begin the 21st century TOGETHER!

End Notes

1. Edgar J. Elliston, citing Orlando Costas, in "Christian Social Transformational Distinctives," *Christian Relief and Development: Developing Workers for Effective Ministry*, edited by E. J. Elliston. Irvin, 1. TX: Word Publishing, 1989. p. 168.

2. John Steward, *Where God, People & Deeds Connect: Biblical Wholism.* Melbourne: World Vision Australia. 1990. p. 6.

3. David Engelhard, "The Lord's Motivated Concern for the Underprivileged," *Calvin Theological Journal.* Vol. 15. No. 1. April 1980. p. 5.

4. Ibid., pp. 6-7.

5. Ibid., pp. 9-10.

6. David J. Bosch. *Transforming Mission: Paradigm Shifts in Theology of Mission.* Maryknoll, NY: Orbis Books, 1991. p. 119.

7. Paul E. Pierson, "Missions and Community Development: A Historical Perspective" in *Christian Relief and Development.* p. 8.

8. Ibid., pp. 10-11.

9. Ibid., p. 11. In Holland, J. Voetius developed the first Protestant missiology already in the 1600s, and remarkably he gave us the three goals of Christian mission—the conversion of sinners, the planting of the church and the changing of society in accord with the Word of God.

10. Sidney H. Rooy, The Theology of Missions in Puritan Tradition (Grand Rapids: Eerdmans, 1965), pp. 316-317. Cited by Pierson, Christian Relief and Development. op. cit., p. 11.

11. Ibid., p. 13.

12. Pierson, op. cit., pp. 13-14.

13. Ibid., p. 14.

14. Ibid., p. 20.

15. Linda Smith, "Recent Historical Perspectives on the Evangelical Tradition," in *Christian Relief and Development*, op. cit., p. 25.

16. Ibid., pp. 25-26.

17. Craig Ellison makes this observation in his chapter, "Addressing Felt Needs of Urban Dwellers," in *Planting and Growing Urban Churches: From Dream to Reality*, edited by Harvie M. Conn (Grand Rapids, MI: Baker book House, 1997), p. 101.

18. Ibid., p. 97.

19. Ibid., p. 98.

20. Op. cit.

21. Op. cit.

22. Bryant Myers, "What is Poverty Anyway?" In MARC Newsletter, number 97-1, March 1997. p. 3.

23. Harv Oostdyk, "Step One: The Gospel and the Ghetto" (Basking Ridge, NJ: SonLife International, 1983), p. 190-191.

24. Op. cit., p. 191.

25. Ibid. p. 191.

26. Douglas Hall, "A View from Boston's Inner City," Transformation, April-June 1991. p. 20.

27. Robert Moffitt, "Wholistic for the Local Church: Curriculum Project Report." Tempe, Arizona. July 1997.

28. Tetsunao Yamamori, *God's New Envoys,* (Portland, OR: Multnomah Press, 1987). pp. 140-141.